Secrets of the Desert

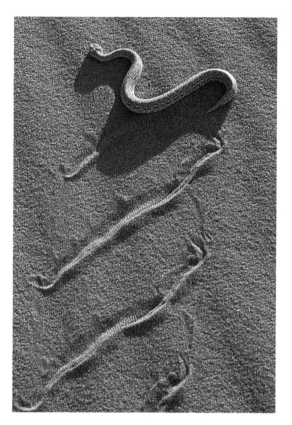

KATH MURDOCH & STEPHEN RAY

For our goddaughter, Matilda Jane Hope, with whom we look forward to sharing many secrets of the Earth.

Written by Kath Murdoch and Stephen Ray
Illustrated by Xiangyi Mo
Designed by Peter Shaw
Picture Research by Brigitte Zinsinger

Published by Mimosa Publications Pty Ltd
PO Box 779, Hawthorn 3122, Australia
© 1995 Mimosa Publications Pty Ltd

Literacy 2000 is a Trademark registered in the
United States Patent and Trademark Office.

Distributed in the United States of America by

Rigby

A Division of Reed Elsevier Inc.
500 Coventry Lane
Crystal Lake, IL 60014
800-822-8661

Published in Canada by
  PEARSON EDUCATION
  26 Prince Andrew Place
  Don Mills
  Ontario M3C 2T8

03 02 01 00
10 9 8
Printed in China through Bookbuilders

ISBN 0 7327 1570 9

Contents

What Are Deserts?

Deserts are places where water is scarce. They have very little rainfall, and most deserts are very hot during the day. In some, the temperature of the ground can sometimes reach as high as 80°C – that's hot enough to burn you. It's hard to imagine how any living thing could survive in such a place.

Some deserts are vast stretches of sand. But other deserts have very little sand. Many have rocky terrain, and deep gullies and canyons.

DESERT DATA: COLD DESERTS?

Antarctica is an extremely cold place. Yet many scientists describe parts of it as desert because no rain has fallen for hundreds of years.

Lots of Life

Animals and plants of the desert have little protection from the sun, and must cope with extreme temperatures and a lack of water. And yet the variety of life that is "at home" in these harsh conditions is enormous: from small bushes to towering cacti.

Scorpion, Great Victoria Desert, Australia

Sand lizard, Namib Desert, Africa

What might have left these tracks?

Sturt's desert pea,
Great Victoria Desert,
Australia

Barrel cactus,
Borrego Desert,
North America

Gemsbok,
Namib Desert,
Africa

7

Many desert creatures have "relatives" that live in places with very different conditions. For example, there are foxes living in the hot, dry environments of deserts, but there are also species of foxes which live in cool areas of Europe. Each species has special features which help it to survive in its habitat.

A desert coyote and a gray wolf are closely "related," but have adapted to very different conditions.

Whose tracks are these?

Although they look very similar, a western bearded dragon and a Boyd's forest dragon live in very different environments.

A desert tortoise and a green sea turtle

Keeping Cool

In the middle of the day, when temperatures are highest, there are few signs of life in the desert. Most animals escape the burning rays of the sun by sheltering in precious patches of shade. Some animals have developed remarkable ways of beating the heat.

Dingoes pant to help keep cool. The rapid movement of air over the tongue helps to cool the animal's blood.

Chameleons, like many desert reptiles, often stand on only two legs. This reduces their contact with the hot ground.

What kind of creature left this track?

DESERT DATA: WHY ARE DAYS SO HOT?

Few clouds form over deserts, and there is very little moisture in desert air. This means that the sun's rays beat straight down, making the ground and the surrounding air very hot.

There is life *beneath* the burning surfaces of many deserts. Shielded from the direct rays of the sun, underground burrows are cool havens for many desert creatures.

The African golden mole is almost completely blind, and uses its sense of touch to find the way in dark underground burrows. ▶

American spadefoot toads spend almost all of their lives under the ground in waterproof sacs. They come to the surface only after heavy rains.

DESERT DATA:
LAYERS OF HEAT

Desert heat is greatest at the surface; above and below ground level the heat is less intense.

300m 27°C

2m 43°C

1m 50°C

Surface 75°C

1.5m 27°C

Some species of termites build cooling structures below their tall nest mounds. They construct rows of thin walls which draw the cooler underground air up into the mound.

Secrets of the Night

There are many changes in the desert at night. Without any clouds to hold in the day's heat, deserts become very cold. Creatures of the day return to burrows, rocks, and bushes for warmth and protection until morning. And nocturnal animals emerge from their hiding places.

Elf owls are highly-skilled nocturnal hunters.

The thick coat of the fennec fox keeps it warm as it hunts in the cold night.

Evening primrose flowers would shrivel and die if they opened in the daytime desert heat. In the cold night, the pale petals attract insects which help to pollinate the plant.

Gerbils come out of their burrows in the cool night.▶

Finding Water

Like all living things, desert plants and animals must have water to survive. But water is usually very scarce in the desert – even years can pass without a drop of rain falling. Desert plants and animals have developed many ways to find and store the water they need for survival.

Some desert beetles collect tiny amounts of water from the air. They position their bodies so that moisture condenses on them and drips toward their mouths.

Many animals get the water they need from their food. A juicy scorpion is a drink as well as a meal for this Australian dunnart.

The baobab tree stores water in its thick trunk.

What made these tracks?

Camels store fat in their humps. The fat can be converted to liquid and energy as the camels need it.

Finding Food

Desert creatures, like all animals, need to eat plants or other animals. But in the desert, plants and animals can be hard to find.

Desert animals make the most of any food available. As well as eating the succulent leaves, stalks, or fruit of plants, many animals eat the seeds and even the bark. Insects and other animals that live in and around desert plants can be food for larger predators, too – all forming part of a complex food web.

Some desert animals eat only occasionally. This sand snake will not need food for several days once it has swallowed the lizard.

When a trapdoor spider senses movement above its trapdoor, it rushes out of its burrow and grabs its prey.

The saguaro cactus of the American Sonoran desert provides food, moisture, and even homes for many desert animals. This desert skyscraper may grow to 15 meters high and live as long as 200 years. Yet it blooms only once a year – for just one night in May.

Many animals, including insects, feast on the flowers and help to pollinate the plant. These plant-eating animals also become food for other animals, such as birds.

Cactus wrens eat insects that are attracted to the saguaro flowers.

The Big Wet

Hot days followed by clear, cold nights form a weather pattern for many deserts. But this pattern can be interrupted by sudden, flooding rains that bring amazing changes to the landscape and the plants and animals of the desert.

Seeds, buried beneath the soil, quickly sprout and take root, and some plants bloom for the first time in months, or even years. For many desert species, a torrential rainfall brings the only chance for their continued survival.

A heavy burst of rain can create crevices and ravines in the landscape.

Hundreds of shield shrimp eggs may hatch in a shallow pool of water. The shrimps grow, mate, and lay their own eggs, which will not hatch until the next big rainfall.

Pink gossypium, like many desert plants, sprouts, grows, flowers, and produces new seeds in the few weeks after a rare downpour. The new seeds will not sprout until the next "big wet."

DESERT DATA: **A LONG DROUGHT**

The Atacama desert in South America has experienced periods of more than 40 years without rain.

Desert Pools

Although there is very little water on the surfaces of deserts, there can be large volumes of *ground water* deep under the surface.

Over thousands of years, rain water which has seeped through the ground can accumulate in porous rocks (rocks with millions of tiny holes) or in buried cracks and caves. These underground water storage places are called *aquifers*.

Sometimes ground water rises to the surface, or near to the surface, forming an *oasis*. An oasis can support an entire community of plants and animals that could not otherwise survive in the desert.

An oasis in the Kerzaz desert, Africa

People in many deserts have developed technology to bring ground water to the surface. These Fulani people in Chad use a well.

In some desert communities there are pump systems to irrigate crops. ▼

People of the Desert

Like desert animals and plants, people living in deserts have many ways of protecting themselves, keeping cool, and finding food and water.

Sometimes this means altering the desert environment to make it more hospitable to humans. As in all places that people change to meet their needs, care is needed to conserve and protect the environment and the natural habitats it provides.

Many desert people wear layers of clothes to insulate them against the heat and to protect them from the sun's burning rays.

Huge amounts of water need to be brought into the deserts to support cities such as Aqaba in Jordan.

Some people in Tunisia beat the heat by building their houses under the ground.

25

Desert Diggings

People have found the fossilized remains of prehistoric plants, animals, and even ancient humans beneath the surfaces of some deserts. From these remains, scientists can see that some deserts were once forests or even oceans.

Mineral deposits lie beneath many parts of the Earth. Huge mines have been dug in deserts to collect oil, diamonds, coal, and uranium. But this kind of activity can destroy the habitats of many animals and plants of the desert.

Diamond mine in Australia

Fossils of ancient sea creatures show that this desert was once part of the ocean floor.

Where Are Deserts?

NORTH AMERICA

Great Basin — — Great Plains

Mojave —

Sonoran —

Chihuahuan —

Nordeste

SOUTH AMERICA

Peruvian —

Atacama —

Monte —

— Patagonian

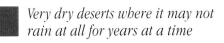 *Very dry deserts where it may not rain at all for years at a time*

 Deserts where there is usually very little rain in a year

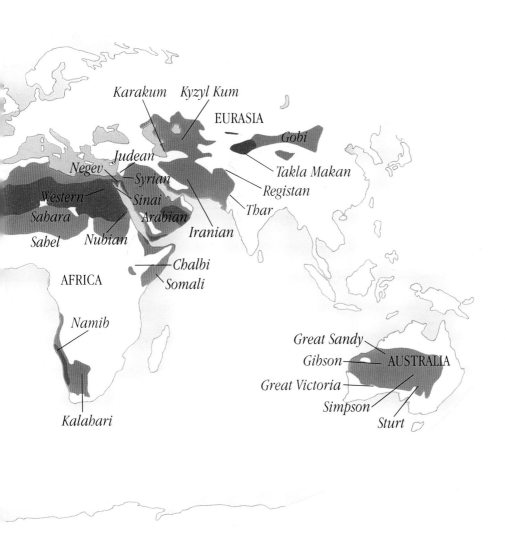

Karakum Kyzyl Kum
EURASIA
Gobi
Judean
Negev
Syrian
Takla Makan
Western
Sinai
Registan
Sahara
Arabian
Thar
Sahel
Nubian
Iranian
Chalbi
AFRICA
Somali
Namib
Great Sandy
Gibson
AUSTRALIA
Great Victoria
Simpson
Kalahari
Sturt

☐ *Deserts which can sometimes receive enough rain to change the land to grassland for part of the year*

Who Made Those Tracks?

Lizard, page 7

Scorpion, page 7

Fox, page 9

Dingo, page 11

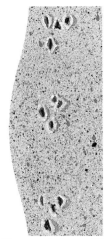

Dunnart, page 17

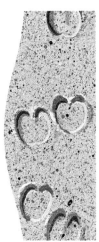

Camel, page 17

Glossary

aquifers   cracks, caves, and porous rocks that hold ground water

cactus   a family of plants which have very juicy stems, spines, and no leaves

ground water   water which has collected under the ground

habitats   environments that plants and animals can live in

irrigation   taking water from one place and using it to water crops in areas that are usually too dry to grow crops

nocturnal animals   animals that are active at night and sleep during the day

oasis   ground water in a desert that has risen to the surface or near to the surface

pollinate   to move pollen from one flower to another. Insects and birds pollinate flowering plants as they eat nectar from the flowers Pollination is necessary for plants to produce fruit and seeds

predators   animals that hunt and kill other animals for food

terrain   the shape of the land and what it is made of

Index

TITLES IN THE SERIES

Photography: *Ardea London: I. R. Beames* (termites, page 13); *Wardene Weisser* (coyote, page 8). *Auscape International: Jeff Foott* (mountainous desert, page 4); *Francois Gohier* (barrel cactus, page 7); *Reg Morrison* (fossils, page 27; scorpion, page 6); *Mark Newman* (saguaro in bloom, page 19); *D. Parer & E. Parer-Cook* (Antarctica page 5; Sturt's desert pea, page 7; baobab tree, page 17); *John Shaw* (cactus wren, page 19). *Australian Picture Library: J. P. & E. S. Bake* (Aqaba, page 25); *J. Carnemolla* (stony desert, page 4); *Leo & Irene Mei* (shield shrimp, page 20); *Leo Meier* (Boyd's forest dragon, page 9; dunnart, page 16; gossypium, page 21); *Jonathon Marks* (wild flowers, page 21); *Gerry Whitmont* (evening primrose, page 15); *F. Zentrale* (sand dunes, page 4-5); (oasis, page 22); (desert irrigation, page 23); (underground dwellings, page 25); (dingo, page 10); (chameleon, pages 10-11). *Brigitte Zinsinger:* (saguaro cactus, page 19). *Bruce Coleman: Erwin & Peggy Bauer* (tortoise, page 9); *Jan Burton* (gerbil, page 15); *Carol Hughes* (beetle, page 16); *David Hughes* (sidewinding adder, page 18); *Austin J. Stevens* (sand lizard, page 6). *Impact: John Evans* (camels, pages 24-25); *Rhonda Klevansky* (Atacama desert, page 21); *Alan Keohane* (floods, page 20). *Oxford Scientific Films: Anthony Bannister* (gemsbok, pages 6-7); *Eyal Bartov* (fennec fox, page 15); *David Cayless* (spadefoot toad, page 12); *Fredrik Ehrenstrom* (snake, page 18); *Michael Fogden* (sidewinding adder, cover); *NHPA: Anthony Bannister* (golden mole, page 12). *Stock Photos: Bob Abraham* (green sea turtle, page 9); *Bill Bachman* (diamond mine, page 26; termite mound, page 13). *The Image Bank: Ronald R. Johnson* (camels, pages 16-17). *The Photo Library: Geoff Higgins* (western bearded dragon, page 9); *Peter Knowles* (trapdoor spider, page 18); *Tom & Pat Leeson* (wolf, page 8); *C. K. Lorenz* (elf owl, page 14); *Jacques Jangoux* (Fulani people, page 22-23).